OCEAN COUNTING
ODD NUMBERS

Jerry Pallotta

Illustrated by Shennen Bersani

 Charlesbridge

Thank you to Pam Giovannini and the Front Street Bookstore, Scituate, Massachusetts.
—J. P.

To my sister, Holly Ann McNeil, with love
—S. B.

Text copyright © 2005 by Jerry Pallotta
Illustrations copyright © 2005 by Shennen Bersani

Published by Charlesbridge
85 Main Street
Watertown, MA 02472
(617) 926-0329
www.charlesbridge.com

Library of Congress Cataloging-in-Publication Data
Pallotta, Jerry.
Ocean counting : odd numbers / Jerry Pallotta ;
illustrated by Shennen Bersani.
p. cm.
Summary: Presents information about a variety of sea creatures,
from one striped bass to 50 blue sharks.
ISBN 0-88106-151-4 (reinforced for library use)
ISBN 0-88106-150-6 (softcover)
1. Counting—Juvenile literature. 2. Marine animals—Juvenile literature.
[1. Marine animals. 2. Counting.] I. Bersani, Shennen, ill. II. Title.
QA113.P35   2004
513.2'11—dc21   98-046035

Printed in China
(hc) 10 9 8 7 6 5 4 3 2 1
(se) 10 9 8 7 6 5 4 3 2 1

Illustrations done in colored pencil on Arches Aquarelle paper
Display type and text type set in Elroy and Caslon 3
Color separated, printed, and bound by R. R. Donnelley
Production supervision by Brian G. Walker
Designed by Susan Mallory Sherman

Striped Bass

This book counts by twos. We are starting with the first odd number, one! One Striped Bass! Sport fishermen love this fish because it can be found near shore. It is a challenge to catch. Striped Bass do not have sharp teeth. Their teeth feel like velcro.

Sunfish

3
three

These three huge Sunfish are strange-looking. They look as if their tails were cut off. Sunfish have a tiny mouth that is shaped like a bird's beak.

Count the five Blood Stars! Should we call them sea stars? Most people call them starfish. Starfish are in a group of animals called echinoderms, which means "rough skin."

Blood Stars

5
five

7
seven

Basking Sharks

These seven Basking Sharks like to swim slowly and bask in the sun. They cruise with their mouth wide open to catch plankton with their gill rakers. Basking Sharks are the second-largest fish in the ocean.

Little Green Crabs

If you go to a beach at low tide, it is easy to find nine
Little Green Crabs. Gently lift a rock and look underneath—
there they are! Skip count! One, three, five, seven, nine!
Are you enjoying odd numbers? Don't be crabby! Keep counting!

Northern Stars

Northern Stars are orange in color.
If a Northern Star loses one of its five legs,
a new one grows in its place. Sometimes the
lost leg grows into a whole new starfish!

Surf Clams

Surf Clams have a hard shell. You can find them if you wade into the surf at a sandy beach during low tide. Here is a secret! Wait for a dead-low tide that comes with a full moon. Then you can walk out to the clams and not get wet.

15
fifteen

Limpets

A Limpet is a single-shelled mollusk that attaches itself to rocks. A Limpet is shaped like a little mountain. Count the fifteen Limpets.

Mackerels

These seventeen Mackerels are doubly camouflaged. A Mackerel's back is blue and its belly is white. If you are looking down into the water from the surface, a Mackerel blends in with the blue ocean. If you are underwater, looking up, the surface of the ocean appears white, just like a Mackerel's belly.

Lumpfish

19
nineteen

Lumpfish have a suction cup on their belly. They do not suck blood; they attach themselves to things so waves won't push them around. Fishermen say it is bad luck to hurt a Lumpfish. You nineteen Lumpfish, it is your lucky day.

Moon Snails

When a Moon Snail comes out of its pretty shell, its body is ten times larger than its shell. The collar you see is made of thousands of its eggs. Count the twenty-one Moon Snails.

23 Horseshoe Crabs

twenty-three

The tails of these twenty-three
Horseshoe Crabs are not weapons.
A Horseshoe Crab uses its tail to flip
itself over if it lands upside down.
A Horseshoe Crab's mouth
is between its legs.

Cunners

Say hello to twenty-five Cunners. Some people call them perch. These fish are difficult to catch. They nibble like crazy and are experts at stealing bait.

Hake

If you pick up some of these twenty-seven Hake, you will notice that they are soft and mushy. These bottom-feeders are also called mud hake, cusks, and whiting.

Mussels

Count these twenty-nine blue Mussels. Not many mollusks have a blue shell. If you ever look for blue sea glass, mussel shells can confuse you.

29
twenty-nine

31
thirty-one

Hermit Crabs

Since Hermit Crabs have a soft, unprotected body, they climb into an empty snail shell and live there. As they grow larger, they move into a larger shell. Would you like to live in a shell? We made it to thirty-one!

Sand Dollars

Yay! Thirty-three! Most people recognize the white bony shells of dead Sand Dollars. The purple Sand Dollars are alive. They make the ocean floor look like it is covered in purple polka dots!

Angel Wings

35
thirty-five

The unusual shape of these clams makes it easy to see why they are called Angel Wings. They have a very thin shell. Be careful—if you touch one, the shell usually breaks. Count the thirty-five Angel Wings.

How can you tell an even number from an odd number? It's easy. Even numbers end with zero, two, four, six, or eight. Odd numbers end with one, three, five, seven, or nine. Don't forget to count the thirty-seven Black Sea Bass.

Black Sea Bass

39
thirty-nine

Skate Eggs

You are walking along a beach and you see these strange, pointy things. What are they? They are thirty-nine Skate Eggs. Skates are a type of ray. Some sharks also have egg cases that look like these.

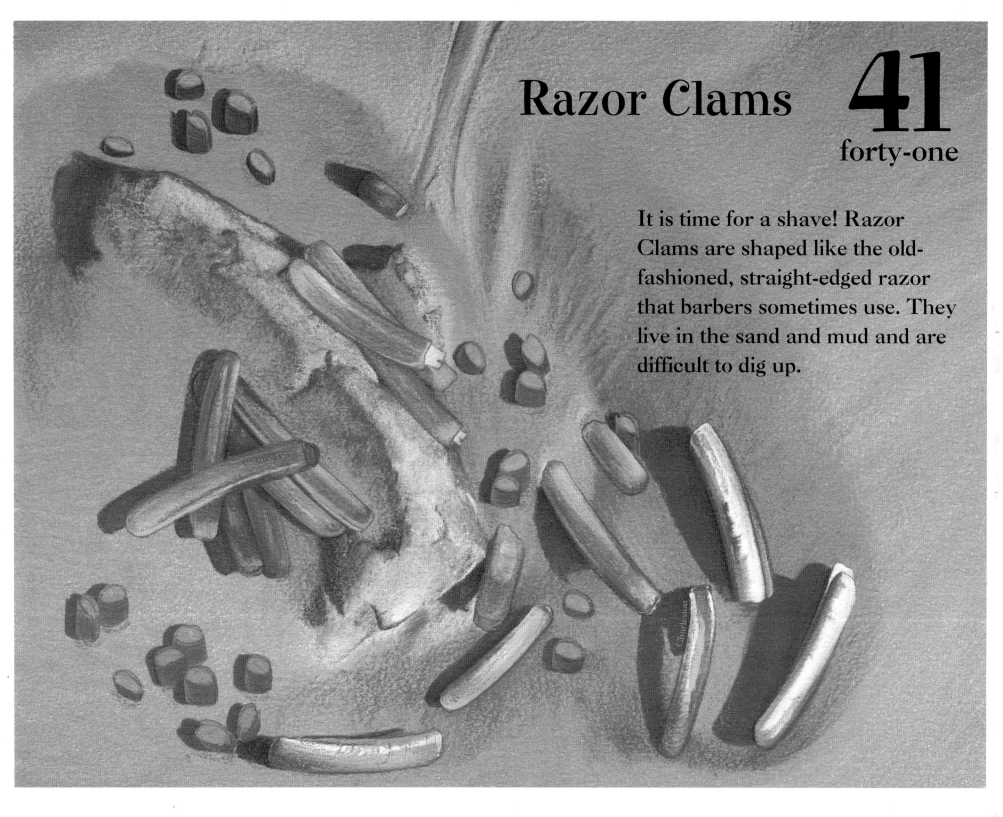

Razor Clams

It is time for a shave! Razor Clams are shaped like the old-fashioned, straight-edged razor that barbers sometimes use. They live in the sand and mud and are difficult to dig up.

43
forty-three

Pollack

Pollack have a stripe across the side of their body. Notice the dorsal fins along the back. One, two, three dorsal fins. Hey, that is an odd number!

Whelks

Welcome to forty-five
Whelks. Whelks are snails
that have a tough, thick shell.
Some Whelks have a shell that spirals to
the left. Other Whelks have a shell that spirals
to the right. Are you a lefty or a righty?

Forty-seven Pipefish fill these two pages. They have been painted their actual size!

47
forty-seven Pipefish

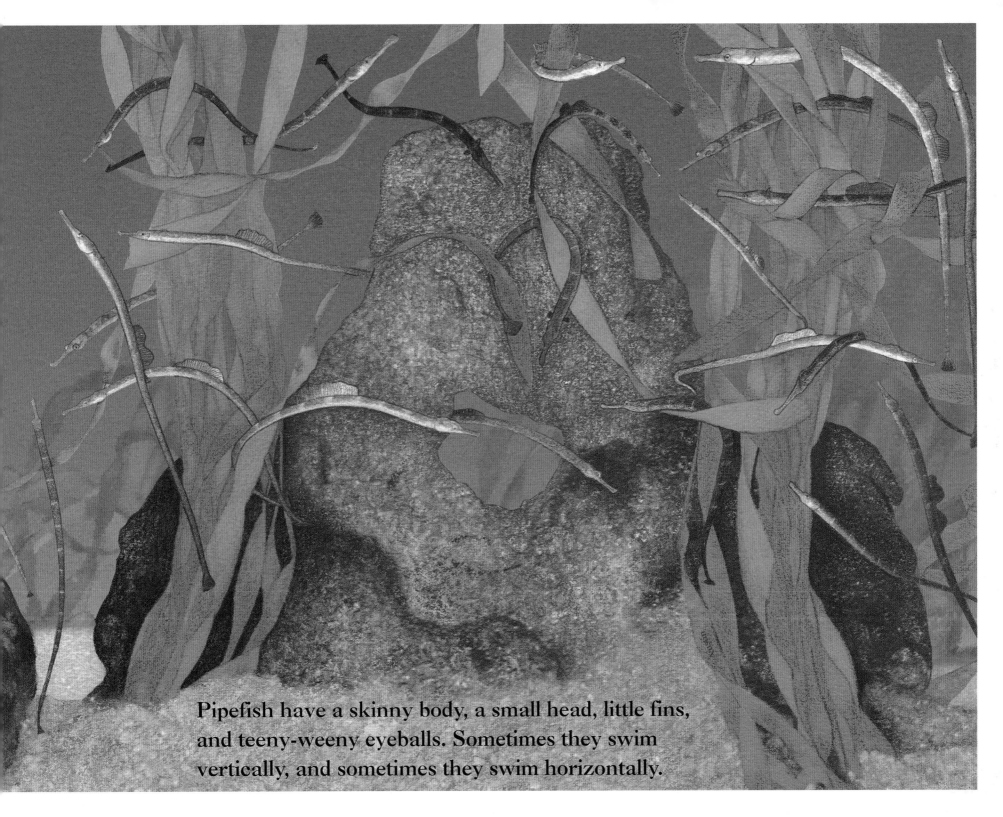

Pipefish have a skinny body, a small head, little fins, and teeny-weeny eyeballs. Sometimes they swim vertically, and sometimes they swim horizontally.

49
forty-nine

Smelts

OK, go! One, three, five, seven, nine, eleven, thirteen, fifteen, seventeen, nineteen, twenty-one, twenty-three, twenty-five, twenty-seven. If you get tired of counting fish, count the eyeballs. Twenty-nine, thirty-one, thirty-three, thirty-five, thirty-seven, thirty-nine, forty-one, forty-three, forty-five, forty-seven, FORTY-NINE!

Forty-nine Smelts! A group of fish is called a school.
Here is a school of Smelts. You have to admit they
have a funny name. Should we say old ones are
smelly Smelts? Or are they Smelts that smell?

Blue Sharks

And if you add one more, we have counted to fifty! Fifty is an even number. Even numbers can be divided into two equal whole numbers. Here are fifty Blue Sharks.

Blue Sharks are known for traveling long distances.
The other fish in this book would probably be happy
if these Blue Sharks just swam away.

O
zero

The Blue Sharks are gone!
The fish, mollusks, crabs,
lobsters, and sea stars are also
gone. Now there are zero
ocean creatures on this page.
Oops, zero is an even number!